How to Become a Professor:

A Non-traditional Guide

By Christopher M. Davis, PhD
http://www.drcmdavis.com

In telling my story, it is important to reference people who have had an important part, especially family, teachers, and colleagues. I have tried to leave names out of it. I am appreciative of everyone who has contributed to my story and for the sake of space, it did not work to mention everyone who has had an influence. I have highlighted a few people, but these are just a small subset of the important people. I have also attempted to leave out the names of the colleges and universities where I have worked since I do not have (and did not seek out) permission to use their names.

For my mother Caroline Jennings and sister Carol Wood and all of the other teachers in our family.

Table of Contents

Overview

Over my twenty plus years in higher education, the career path for professors has undergone a significant transition. When I was in grad school at the University of Michigan in the early 1990s, most doctoral graduates would apply for full-time positions doing some combination of teaching and research. While some career schools used part-time faculty, most of these faculty did not have terminal degrees and the schools focused on students in associate degree programs.

By the time I started teaching as an adjunct faculty member a few year later, things were starting to change. Career colleges were beginning to expand their offerings into bachelor's and graduate school. Online degree programs began to emerge that allow many working adults access to higher education.

At the same time, traditional higher education including state supported public institutions and private non-profits began to face a succession of financial challenges. As budgets tightened, the number of traditional track positions began to shrink, leading to even traditional schools hiring more and more part-time faculty.

Traditional doctoral programs continued to produce the same number of graduates even as traditional opportunities decreased. Non-traditional universities added even more newly minted PhDs as they received accreditation for new doctoral programs.

While some still succeed at the traditional path and land a coveted position at a traditional university or at least a full-time teaching position somewhere, many do not. Even those who do land on the tenure track are not guaranteed of tenure and may find themselves on the academic job market again in seven years.

Those who do not land a full-time position may find a temporary and/or part-time position or positions. Some will give the job market another try each spring iring season. Others quit on academics, joining those who started an alternative academic" career right out of grad school.

your goal is a traditional higher education career path of going to graduate chool for ten years and then applying for tenure track positions at a similar nstitution, this book is probably not going to help you very much. In the ompanion web site I do recommend other resources that can help. I wish you ne best of luck, because no matter how hard you work, how smart you are, or ven how pretty you are, the odds are against you.

Vhile I did attend a traditional research university for graduate school, my areer in higher education has been very non-traditional, and the experience nd advice have to share is likewise non-traditional. In addition to my own xperience, I have been an administrator in multiple institutions and worked ith thousands of faculty.

he audience I am writing for are people who usually have some years of rofessional experience. They have family and commitments that do not allow em to relocate to some university town and live the graduate student life for a ecade. My audience has experience and knowledge that they would like to hare with others that is both academic and grounded in the real world.

he truth of the matter is that the traditional higher education job market is usy right now and likely to get worse. Graduate programs continue to produce s many or more doctoral students while enrollment at traditional schools ecrease. If your dream is a traditional higher ed teaching position as glorified n many movies, you should strongly consider revising your dream into a less aditional career path...in which case this book might be very helpful.

you did earn your PhD whether from a traditional research university or one f the newer non-traditional programs and now find yourself challenged to find teaching position, then this book should help you understand how to break to teaching outside of the traditional career path of tenure track positions.

his book has six chapters while you can read them in order, depending in your terests and experience, you may want to skip to specific chapters while avoiding others. I have provided overviews of each chapter so that you can make an informed decision on what to skip.

Chapter One: My Story

The story of how I became a professor is a long one, but I think it helps to understand the source of my advice. Feel free to skip ahead if this is not your cup of tea. I offer it only has context for why you should pay attention to the res of this book.

Chapter Two: Preparing for the Journey

I started this project out of a desire to help others realize the dream of becoming a professor while avoiding some of the pitfalls I have seen others make. This chapter is for people who are still thinking about higher education teaching as a career and need to know about requirements and other background information. Others who are trying to make a go of it might also find some value in reviewing this chapter.

Chapter Three: Finding and Landing a Teaching Job

This chapter is dedicated to anyone who is looking for their first or their next teaching job. The advice here focuses on part-time teaching opportunities and many full-time positions at less traditional institutions. At traditional research universities and those colleges that strive to emulate research universities, the hiring process is very different. Most searches are nationwide and involve a formal structure of multiple interviews with a hiring committee. These positions are also few and in high demand. If you are focused on these positions, this chapter will not help you. Instead seek out advice from your graduate advisor. you do not have a graduate advisor because you attended a non-traditional school or you have been out of graduate school for some time or do not have a doctorate, then you probably have minimal opportunity at this type of position. You will want to look at how to land a part-time teaching job that might eventually lead to a full-time opportunity. (Realistically, though, probably not.)

Chapter Four: Making the Most of Your Shot

you have your first (or a current) teaching job, this chapter will tell you how to make the most of that opportunity to get called back to teach again. It will also e helpful if you want to leverage your part-time gig into a full-time position with enefits. I will also address signs it is time to fire yourself (or the school you are eaching for).

Chapter Five: Career Advice for Future Professors

n addition to my perspective, I share with you results from a survey on advice or those interested in becoming a faculty. I also share some of the most nportant published articles published in the higher education literature on this opic.

Chapter Six: The Independent Professor

s I have worked on this project over the last couple of years, I have identified n opportunity for professors to share their knowledge outside of traditional olleges and publishers as an independent professor. Many people with less redentials and experience than you are making money with online teaching nd publishing, why not you? Read this chapter to learn more.

Companion Website

Things change online frequently. Links die or become porn sites. New sites are orn. Rather than include links and references that can go out of date, I have nstead created a companion web site. Access is free, and you can share the nk with anyone who is interested.

How to Become a Professor Web site:
ttps://www.drcmdavis.com/p/how-to-become-professor.html

Chapter One: My Story

My journey to become a professor begins when I was younger (ninth grade maybe) I wanted be a writer. One evening my mother (who did not always frequently offer advice) told me that I should do something that was going to make money…like be a lawyer. My mother's family had had a hard time growing up in the Depression, and her years married to my father and raising my older siblings had not always been easy. She had appreciation for the valu of money and security. For reasons I no longer recall, I took her suggestion an ran with it.

For the next three years of high school, I was on the debate team. If speech and theater had been varsity sports, I would have lettered in four different sports. I enjoyed these activities, but my goal was to go to law school and become a lawyer. Not a criminal defense lawyer like Perry Mason, or even a prosecutor or any sort of trial lawyer like you might see on television. I had my sights set on corporate law, because I believed that to be where the money was.

College - The Undergraduate Years

In September of 1986, I headed off to the University of Michigan with a plan to major in economics with the ultimate goal of becoming a filthy rich corporate lawyer to make my mother proud. All of my plans were derailed within the first month. That summer I had started dating a lovely and sweet young woman who had one year left in high school before she would be hopefully joining me at the University. Unfortunately, she fell for someone else who was also still in high school and broke my heart. I have mostly gotten over this now, and we ar friends in Facebook, and I don't think it would have worked out eventually and maybe she just saw it first. I did not realize this thirty years ago. Then I had the epiphany that I could not be guaranteed in life that I would find someone who would make me happy, and that I had better make sure I did something for a living that was going to make me happy. I did not think that being a corporate ttorney was necessarily going to do that. That is when I decided to become a rofessor.

n hindsight, this should not be surprising. My mother was a teacher. One of my isters was a teacher. My mother's parents including her step-mother and two f her sisters were teachers. One of my mother's grandmothers had been a eacher. Education was the family business. At the time I was taking intensive atin. My Latin professor was a Virgil scholar and loved teaching students atin. My interest in Latin was that it was the simplest way to fulfill my foreign anguage requirement, and because it was the intensive version, it was taught y a full-professor. Inspired by this professor I decided to become a professor f classics. I loved Roman history, because when Roman politicians did omething stupid and bad for Rome, it was 2000 years in the past versus ontemporary leaders of the free world who still did stupid things that were bad or the country but with consequences that could be felt today.

My mother was not happy, not that she shared this with me. Again, she was not ne for offering advice. I decided I need a weekend away from campus, so I vent to visit my Dad. My parents had divorced when I was a year old, and he ffered a safe haven to try to get over my still broken heart. Dad gave advice bout as frequently as my Mom, so his advice that trip stands out. He told me ow he wished he had gone back to university when my Mom divorced him to tudy for a graduate degree in history and become a professor. If he had, my)ad would have been about 43 when he started his graduate education and in is 50s by the time he finished his degree. It was not a realistic idea, but that vas typical for my Dad. His lesson, though, was that he thought what I was loing was a great idea and he supported me even if my Mom did not.

My schedule was loaded with courses like Latin and Greek for my second year t Michigan, but first I needed to finish my second semester of intensive Latin.)r. Ross had turned the class over to a newer member of the faculty, which vas fine. What was not so good was the mystery illness that put me in the ospital for the week after spring break. Before you start speculating on what I lid for spring break, let me explain that I stayed on campus working in the afeteria. I think I may have been exposed to some cleaning chemicals that did number on my liver. I had been taking 6 classes that semester, and after missing a week of class, I thought I should cut down, so I dropped one class. The problem with parents who do not give advice is that no one tells you when you should take it easy. The doctors also failed to inform me that I could expect to be sick including fatigue for as long as the next year. My grade in Latin went from an A- first semester to a D+ the second. I remembered that languages were not really my thing. Maybe classics was not a great idea for me.

That summer I stayed in Ann Arbor (I did not want to return to the source of my broken heart), and I worked in the cafeteria and took an intro psychology course. We had two graduate assistants who were team teaching the course. One of them included a section on social psychology. My life was forever changed. Reading about Asch's conformity experiments, Milgram's work on authority, and Zimbardo's prison experiment on role theory opened my eyes to a new understanding of why people do the things that they do. This I had to learn.

The courses in Greek were gone. (I still had to manage through one last Latin class to finish the language requirement.) Instead I loaded up on psychology and sociology. My plan was to double major in both, because I was fascinated by the intersection of individual behavior and group and social influences. Psychology was (and probably still is) a popular major, and to be admitted to the honor's psychology program, you had to apply. Sociology, on the other hand, was happy to take anyone who wanted to take the honor's track. One of the things that I had learned from Dr. Ross in Latin is that people will tend to do whatever is easiest. He applied this principle to linguistics and why words were pronounced the way that they were. It also explains why I applied to the honor's sociology program and not psychology.

Second semester of my sophomore year was looking up. After a liver biopsy, the doctor's pronounced me healed from my mystery illness. My heart was still broken, and then it was broken harder. Again at the end of spring break my mother called to let me know that my older brother (the one closest to me in age) had been struck and killed by a drunk driver. At least I was studying things I enjoyed, which gave me something to focus on during the depression that followed. (No one realized that I was depressed, and I did not until years later. Maybe I should have taken more psychology courses.) I took a class in merican sociology. In this class, we studied issues of social stratification in ie U.S. and also American influence in other countries during the Cold War. or anyone who is concerned about how college corrupts young minds, I was lready corrupted. I had abandoned my Republican parents for the Young emocrats while in junior high school. For those of you who think that most ollege professors are leftists, I no longer support the Democrats. Or the .epublicans. But more importantly, I think it is in appropriate for me to share iy personal political views in the classroom. A good academic focuses on data nd ideas from an objective perspective in our role in the classroom. As private itizens we have the same rights as everyone else to support the ideas and ssues that we believe in.

nyway, as an honor's student, I needed to write a thesis. One day after class I vas talking to my professor about this, and he mentioned that in 1911 the ocialists had elected a mayor and two aldermen in Flint, Michigan. My parents vere from the greater Flint area. We had never been taught in school this ecret history of socialists holding office in America. Keep in mind that this was t the height of the Reagan presidency and the height of the Cold War when ocialists and their communist cousins were the enemies of all Americans. I sed an independent study that summer to start researching the topic. I also vorked on a couple of different research projects coding surveys and entering ata. As a result of my hard work, I was positioned to finish my undergraduate tudies with only one more year. That summer I also met my college weetheart.

hat September (1988), I wanted to take a graduate sociology course on istorical sociology, but the course had no room. Near the department offices, I aw a flyer for a course in gaming/simulation design taught in the urban lanning department. I called the professor, and he said to come to the course) see if I would be interested. (Games had always been a hobby and interest f mine, so this looked really interesting.) The focus of the course was to esign a game for a client, Women's Action for Nuclear Disarmament (WAND). .gain, these were the days when we all thought nuclear war was a real threat nd possibility. WAND wanted a game that would educate people on mutual ecurity to help mobilize people to support strategies that were not encouraging nutually assured destruction. The following summer, I was hired to finish the game and prepare the project for use. It must have worked, because it was the next year that the USSR collapsed and the Berlin Wall came down.

College: The Graduate School Years

I loved the study of sociology, but my problem was that it was too academic. It identified problems, but it had limited capacity for finding solutions. Urban Planning offered a type of applied sociology. It aimed to apply theories and ideas about people and society to create more livable and effective communities. So for graduate school, I applied to the Master's of Urban Planning. It also meant that I could pursue a Certificate in Gaming and Simulation Studies. I also had the problem that because I finished my undergraduate degree a year early, I did not have the usual time to apply to graduate programs at other universities. Plus, I had a girlfriend who had another year left in her degree. (Remember how that worked for me the last time.)

After one year in the Master's of Urban Planning, I realized that Urban Plannin was too focused on the practical, and that what I wanted was a doctorate so I could become a professor. That goal had not changed. I was accepted into the Urban, Technological, and Environmental Planning program at Michigan. I never finished the master's. I just moved into the doctoral program. The program itself was interdisciplinary. I was required to take graduate courses from across the university. Being able to sample courses and professors from across the offerings of a place like the University of Michigan is a rare opportunity. I made the most of it.
My girlfriend was a Near Eastern and North African Studies major, but she worked in information technology at the university. She taught me a great deal and helped me land a series of part-time positions until we both became consultants for the university working on the helpdesk. Computers were another long-time interest of mine. I had learned to program Fortran 77 on punch cards) when I was 12. I lived in two worlds. One was my graduate study in planning, where I looked at organizations and how they processed information, and another when I worked with computers and helped others

olve their problems. It was one of my professors who opened my eyes to the connection between those two worlds. I decided to focus my studies on computers and organizations.

Exile in the Working World

In January 1992, my girlfriend had become my wife. She had finished her master's degree and was working full-time for the university. I was finishing my third year of graduate school and almost done with my coursework. I had a half-time position with the university. A request went out for consultants to work on a special project. The university was a member of a consortium working on a large grant from NASA to make data and information about human change available over the Internet. The Cold War was over, and the new global concern was climate change. The Internet was not well-known outside of universities and even there only to a few. But that was of course about to change. We volunteered and over the next four months provided IT support to this new organization based not too far from my hometown. They offered us full-time positions, and I was also offered a full-time research fellowship to work on my dissertation. I was told I could only pick one. I picked the job. My thinking was that while I knew about academics and universities, my teaching and research would be better with some real-world experience. In hindsight, I have never been so right. One of my professors warned me not to go, that no one ever comes back and finishes. He was never so wrong, but it took me years to prove that.

The work was exciting. I started in IT, moved to marketing, back to IT in a management position. Was promoted to senior management while still in my 30s. I was moved to government relations where I worked with organizations from around the world, and even presented at a United Nations conference. I had a front row seat to the emergence of the World Wide Web. I learned a lot. I slowly worked away at my doctoral requirements. I finished one last stats class. I did my preliminary exams and achieved candidacy. Or as it is commonly known, I was "all but dissertation (ABD)". I even moonlighted as an assistant high school theater director for three years at my old high school. The problem with full-time employment is that you become accustomed to the lifestyle of a full-time salary. I changed jobs to apply what I knew about technology and building partnerships to a community health care project. When that did not work out, I started my own business doing consulting.

Professor at Last

One of my projects was offering Internet and Web training in partnership with a local, nonprofit college. This college was my first exposure to a college that focused on adult students and career programs. Having spent a few years in the professional world, I valued the practical and applied approach that was very different than my experience at Michigan. Then one day at lunch, I received a call from the Dean asking me if I wanted to teach for the college. The courses were introductory computer courses (Lotus 123 and Microsoft Access). They were offered at a satellite campus about an hour away. I had finally become a professor (or at least a college instructor).

Those courses led to more part-time teaching opportunities at the college. About a year into my adjuncting, the college had an opening for a full-time department chair. I had a successful business, but I remembered that this was always what I wanted to do. I landed the job with the requirement that I had to finish my degree within the next year. That type of requirement is the best motivation to finish, and I did.

Before I finished though, I became Interim Dean, and then permanent Dean. I developed a new program on web design. At the college, deans taught, so I was still in the classroom, in addition to my administrative responsibilities. The college was (and is) a large multi-campus system. At the time, it was growing a all of its locations, and I was interested in learning what was the secret sauce that drive this success. When the position of Director of Instructional Technology open at the corporate offices, I leapt at the opportunity to see what was going on behind the scenes. In the interview, I was asked about how I felt about giving up teaching, but the truth was that I never stopped. I started eaching for the online division in 2000 and transitioned the web design rogram to the online format.

Journey to the Dark Side - Administration

My day job was to help faculty integrate technology into their classes. I managed our interactive video courses. I designed and oversaw the mplementation of our first smart classrooms. I trained faculty on Blackboard nd PowerPoint. I also realized that technology without purpose does not mprove teaching or learning. I proposed re-branding my department as Effective Teaching and Learning. My training expanded to other topics like ollaborative learning, active learning, and assessment.

n time, I was moved to Director of Assessment to lead the implementation of ur student learning assessment program. I also became our Accreditation Liaison Officer with our regional accreditor. In 2004, I became a peer reviewer or our accreditor, and in the years since have visited or otherwise worked with a variety of institutions across the region.

was very fortunate to have great mentors at Baker who helped me become an effective administrator. In 2008, I took this experience to the bright lights and big city of Chicago to be Vice Provost of Institutional Effectiveness at a university there. From there, I moved to be Vice Provost at a for-profit university. My first role was leading the online faculty and related services like faculty training and scheduling. My second role was leading the doctoral programs.

From there, I headed to Phoenix and a small online university. Over four years here I have moved from Vice President of Institutional Effectiveness to Provost and now President. Becoming a university president has been one of my goals since the start of my higher ed career. Unfortunately, my responsibility is to see the closing of the university.

Why This Book

I do not know what my next step will be. Some days I question whether I shoul stay in higher ed. I and hope that my years of experience allow me to offer some advice to others who like me think that they want to be a professor. The most frequently asked question I would receive from my doctoral students was how to become a professor. I have also had many colleagues seek out advice about how to land a teaching position or advance their career. This book is my response to them and others like them that have a dream of becoming a professor.

Originally, I developed an online course on this topic. The course is still there and will always be free. I wanted to create a book as a way to reach a wider audience. There are some resources in the course such as academic job boar links that I will not seek to replicate in this book as these can change frequently. Instead, I will provide references to the online course so that readers can access the most current information I have to offer.

Chapter Two: Preparing for the Journey

you are just thinking about becoming a professor and researching how to
ecome one, this chapter will help you think through that decision and what you
eed to do next. If you are actively searching for teaching positions, especially
you have not had much success, this chapter might help you identify
pportunities to strengthen your job search.

Why do you want to be a professor?

have hired many faculty and supervised directly or indirectly thousands of
aculty online and in physical classrooms over the last twenty plus years. When
hire faculty, one of my main interests is why they want to be a professor. This
s important for hiring administrators, but you should also have a clear
nderstanding of your own motivations before you pursue this path.

*Do you seek the glory and fame of being the sage on the stage imparting your
wisdom to a classroom full of eager minds?*

> The reality is that teaching is a lonely profession. The professor is alone
> in the classroom with students who often won't appreciate the lessons
> offered until years later. Teaching is not typically a pathway to becoming
> famous. Good faculty focus on their students and not themselves.
> Faculty who are motivated by ego are rarely effective in the classroom.

Have you heard of professors who make six figures with summers off?

> Several years ago, a colleague of mine was featured in a newspaper
> article about how she was earning over a $100,000 a year teaching
> part-time for several online universities. These results are atypical, and
> it is unrealistic to think that this type of productivity is sustainable for
> most. Tenured professors at research universities can make significant
> money, but only after years of teaching and research at lower salaries
> with no guarantees they will be promoted.

Most faculty could probably earn more money an hour working at a fast food restaurant. A typical salary for teaching a 10-week course is about $1,500. You can expect to spend 4 hours a week in the classroom, 8 hours a week preparing for each class, 15 hours each week grading papers (that's only 30 minutes per student), and another 3 hours on office hours and communication with students. That works out to 30 hours a week, 300 hours for the course, or $5/hour.

Do you want to save the world?

Maybe you had a professor who made a difference in your life, and you want to give back in kind. Teaching at any level is a way to make a difference but realize that you will probably have a profound impact on only a few students over an entire career. Saving the world will not be a sustainable motivation in regular grind of teaching.

What are you passionate and knowledgeable about?

In my experience, the faculty who are successful and have sustained job satisfaction are those who have a topic that they are passionate about and want to share with others. I have been blessed to have colleagues who have taught everything from accounting and aviation to composition and world studies. The greater the passion each had for their subject and sharing their passion and knowledge with others, the greater their impact on the students.

If you want to be a professor, the starting point is to determine what do you have a passion for that you would like to share with others? While fame and money can be elusive goals, it can be incredibly rewarding to share your passion and knowledge with others.

Becoming a professor is not easy, and if your purpose is not strong enough, you will likely give up along the way. Also, understanding your own motivation will help you determine what type of institution matches your goals.

Types of Higher Education Institutions

you want to start a career as a professor, it helps to understand the different types of higher education institutions. The qualifications for faculty will vary depending on the mission and student body served by an institution.

Research Universities

The first college in the United States was Harvard, and even today it is one of the first institutions that people think of with its ivy colored walls and fresh-faced students. Harvard and other universities both public and private serve only a small fraction of students. The primary focus of these institutions is not on teaching but on research. Faculty earn tenure based on their research and ability to attract external funding for that research. Classes are taught primarily by graduate students. Professors in the institutions are almost exclusively hired from the ranks of new graduates from similar universities. Unless you are graduating from one of these institutions, you have little chance...and even if you do, there are more applicants than openings.

Private Liberal Arts Colleges

As the United States was settled, hundreds of liberal arts colleges were started, most tied to a religious denomination. Today many of these colleges are struggling in the face of declining enrollments. These colleges tend to put teaching before research, and most classes are taught by full-time faculty with doctoral degrees. To reduce costs, some colleges have started to hire more part-time faculty. The focus in these institutions are undergraduate, liberal arts courses, and if you have a doctorate in the humanities, social sciences, or natural sciences, you might find an opportunity at one of these colleges. Unfortunately, these types of institutions are under significant competitive pressure, and many are closing or merging with other schools. Most faith-based institutions follow the private liberal arts college model to greater and lesser degrees. Some remain very connected to their faith and history while others are much more secular.

Public Colleges and Universities

In addition to public research universities (often known as "flagships"), each state has its own network of public colleges and universities. Like liberal arts colleges, most classes are taught by doctorally prepared faculty who work for the institution full-time. Also, like liberal arts colleges, many are starting to hire part-time faculty to reduce expenses. Unlike liberal arts colleges, many of them have professional programs in addition to liberal arts courses. Many of these colleges began as "normal schools" in the early twentieth century, focused on training school teachers.

Community Colleges

Community colleges emerged in the 1960s to provide access to higher education in local communities. Community colleges offer two year programs (associate degrees). Many students at a community college are traditional-aged students just out of high school who plan to transfer to a four-year college to finish their education. Many community colleges also offered a variety of career programs including truck driving and welding to accounting and culinary arts. Community colleges offer low tuition rates, and though they receive public funding, they employ a large number of part-time faculty to keep costs down and to teach in career programs. Community colleges do not usually require faculty to hold doctoral degrees. While a bachelor's degree is acceptable, most faculty have a master's degree.

Career Schools

Career schools are colleges that have career programs like a community college but without transfer programs for students to continue their studies at a university. Career colleges can be nonprofit or for-profit. In either case, they tend to hire primarily part-time faculty. Colleges that offer undergraduate degrees typically only require a master's degree for faculty, but they also put a priority on professional work experience.

Satellite Campuses / Off-campus Locations

Some larger schools will have satellite campuses in other communities or offer courses at off-campus locations. Depending on the school, these locations can operate with varying amounts of autonomy from the main campus. Sometimes the requirements for faculty will be less than what is required on the main campus, and even the programs may be different.

Online Colleges and Universities

When I started teaching online in 2000, there were few online colleges and universities, and most were branches of brick and mortar colleges. In the years since, most colleges and universities have added one or more online programs. Online courses are the ultimate convenience for working adults who value the ability to study at the time and place that fits their schedule rather than being at a specific place at a set time. Today, some schools are exclusively online. Traditional faculty have been slow to embrace online courses, and often colleges and universities hire part-time faculty to staff these courses. At the same time, many traditional schools are offering new online programs.

How does the type of institution influence hiring?

If you are looking for a full-time position in higher education, knowing what type of institution you are interested in will help you determine what qualifications that you need. For traditional universities and liberal arts colleges, a doctoral degree from a traditional, residential university is typically required. In institutions that employ large numbers of part-time faculty, full-time hires are typically drawn from the part-time faculty.

If you are looking for a part-time teaching opportunity, you will want to start with schools within your local area. This is even true if you are looking for online teaching opportunities. While online schools can and will hire beyond their local area, locals will often have an advantage. It is easier for a local faculty member to come to campus for meetings and other activities. My recommended approach for landing a teaching position is through networking, and it is much easier to network locally than at a distance. Finally, the competition for openings at online universities is national in scope. The university has more opportunities to be selective in who they hire.

What qualifications are required to be a professor?

In large part, the qualifications required to be a professor vary with the type of institution. The rule of thumb is that a professor should have a degree one level higher than the course being taught. In other words, courses in an associate degree program should be taught by someone with at least a bachelor's degree, courses at the bachelor's level require at least a master's degree, and graduate courses should be taught by someone with a terminal degree in that discipline. Typically, it will be hard to find a higher ed teaching position without a master's degree.

What is a terminal degree in a discipline can be interpreted in different ways. Usually this means a doctoral degree such as a Doctor of Philosophy (PhD) or Doctorate of Education (EdD) or Doctorate of Business Administration (DBA). In law, the JD is considered the terminal degree. In fine arts (music, creative writing, painting, etc.), the Master of Fine Arts (MFA) is the terminal degree. In some fields, it is unclear what the terminal degree is. I have not seen any truck driving programs past the associate degree, unless you are including programs in logistics. Paramedics have an associate degree, but I have not found any bachelor degree programs in this specific aspect of healthcare, but emergency medicine is certainly a related area of study.

A historical note...a Doctorate of Philosophy is not just for philosophers. The tradition in higher education is that someone who has studied at the highest level and produced a work of original scholarship (a dissertation) has contributed to the body of knowledge in the discipline and is a doctor. At

Harvard, the faculty of the College of Arts and Sciences has long felt that they alone had the right to grant PhDs, so the College of Education at Harvard developed the Doctorate in Education (EdD) and the College of Business the Doctorate of Management (DM). Many would argue that these latter two degrees are more applied than the PhD, but my personal view is that there are PhDs that are more applied than some EdDs. Some universities offer both. I think the differences are academic, but then we are talking about academics.

Sometimes a college will use professional experience in the place of education. This varies a great deal, and this is more likely in programs where the program is aligned to a specific career or professional outcome. If you are teaching someone auto mechanics, it is more important that you know how to fix cars yourself than what degree you have, and the same is true for other professions. Book learning is seldom a replacement for hands on, practical experience.

What the degree is in is also important. The standard is that someone should have 18 graduate credits in the field being taught. Having an MBA might not be sufficient to teach college-level accounting if one did not take 18 credits in accounting as part of the degree or in additional study. As with other requirements, this can be interpreted in widely different ways. While an MBA might not be enough for accounting, it might be enough to qualify to teach marketing or management. This is another place where professional experience can be a deciding factor. An MBA combined with a decade of experience in accounting should be sufficient qualifications for teaching undergraduate accounting.

A common mistake I have seen people make is earning a doctorate in education. This could be in higher education or in curriculum or in any other focus. If your goal is teaching in higher education, avoid these degrees. (I have taught in such a program, and it was great for people who were working in higher education administration and looking to move up the ladder.) For someone who wants to teach, an education degree only qualifies you to teach education courses. The problem is that most education courses are for K12 teachers, and universities want faculty who also have K12 experience. Unless you are a K12 teacher or administrator looking to move into higher education, stay away from education programs.

If you already have a master's degree and it is related to an area where you have professional experience, then you have the basic qualifications to teach undergraduate courses in that area. A doctorate in that area will make you more attractive to universities, but you do not need the doctorate at institutions that primarily serve undergraduate institutions.

If you have a master's degree but it is not related to the area where you have professional experience, it will be harder to get interviews let alone job offers. If you have a graduate degree in English or Mathematics, you should be able to find a teaching opportunity, regardless of work experience. If you need additional credits in the area you want to teach, you do not need a second master's degree. You just need the magic 18 credits.

Professional credentials and certifications can also be used in place of some degrees. A Certified Public Accountant (CPA) will always be welcome to teach undergraduate accounting even without a master's degree. In information systems, professional certifications may even be required. Healthcare fields may also require faculty to hold licensure or certification.
Universities should not like to hire their own graduates. If your dream job is teaching at Acme University, the last place you want to pursue your doctorate is Acme University. It will often be much harder to get hired from within then as an outsider. Hiring from within means that the program is not bringing in people with new ideas and perspectives. When I ran a doctoral program, many of my students wanted to know how to get hired to teach by the University, and I had to explain that that was not likely to happen. If you truly have your heart set on a specific place, research where the current faculty came from, and go there to study.

It used to be that to study for a doctorate, the only option was to attend a research University as a graduate student. These programs were (and are) designed to be full-time, residential experiences. Often graduate students are employed as teaching or research assistants. Classes are taught during the day, and it is difficult to participate in these programs and have a full-time, professional career off-campus. These programs still exist, and for many universities, in order to be considered for a faculty position (especially full-me), you will need to graduate from one of these programs. The downside is that the typical time to earn one of these degrees can be as much as ten years.

Over the last twenty years, though, non-traditional universities have been approved to offer doctoral programs as well. Many of these are online or offer courses in the evenings or on weekends. There maybe residencies where students meet together for a week at key points in the program, but in general these programs are designed for working adults. This is a great way to earn a doctorate and it will open opportunities for higher ed teaching. I used to run a program like this, and I had a few students who were able to land tenure track teaching positions at traditional colleges. Typically, though, the more prestigious the university you want to teach at, the less likely that a degree from a non-traditional school will be valued. Quality varies widely by program and school, so you will want to do your homework carefully.

In traditional higher education, faculty are involved in research as well as (and often more than) teaching. For full-time positions in research universities, this is still true. In those cases, new faculty are hired typically as freshly minted PhDs from similar institutions. In some fields, new PhDs are expected to first serve in one or more post-doctoral research positions. In most non-research institutions, you are being hired to teach, and unless you will be teaching at the doctoral level, there will be little interest in your research and publications. This (as with everything) may vary. Some colleges may want to hire part-time faculty with research experience, but most places are more concerned with your degrees, professional experience, and ability to be successful in the classroom.

The pecking order of prestige in higher education has meant that many colleges attempt to emulate the big research universities. As a result, even institutions that operationally are focused on teaching, may emphasize scholarship in faculty hiring. Or they may emphasize it in full-time faculty hiring and hire part-time adjunct faculty to do the bulk of the teaching.

Should you pursue a doctorate?

A doctorate (PhD, DBA, EdD, etc.) offers multiple benefits. It also requires a great deal of work, much of it not glamorous, and can cost thousands and thousands of dollars in tuition, and requires a significant sacrifice of time away from faculty, friends, and having a life. If you are not strongly motivated for earning the degree, you will not be successful and should not start. So what are the benefits?

First Benefit – The Credential: The doctorate signifies a few things. Most of all is a credential that demonstrates that the holder invested significant time to earn the degree. Most who start will not finish. Most who finish will take years to get there. (It took me nine years, and I was the first in my class to finish.) This credential is mainly only important in higher education where a doctorate can be a requirement for teaching positions and academic leadership positions

Second Benefit – Research: A doctoral program also means that you have completed a piece of original research resulting in the dissertation. The dissertation is what usually prevents people from finishing. The work is done solo, and it can be challenging to make the time to conduct the research and write up the results. If the faculty advising you are less than helpful, then this process is even more challenging. The ability to conceive and deliver a research project has application beyond higher education.

Third Benefit – Advanced Coursework: A doctoral program also requires course work beyond the master's degree. While this includes research methods and related studies, it can also include additional coursework in the field. This provides some benefit to pursuing a doctorate, a second master's degree can also achieve the same result.

In summary, the primary benefits beyond personal achievement to earning a doctorate are the experience in research and writing and the qualification for a academic career in higher education. The research experience can be addressed with less time, energy, and money, so the real reason to pursue a doctorate is a career in academics.

Much like a hunting license, the doctorate is not a guarantee of success. It is just the price for admission. Traditional higher education has been producing more doctorates than full-time faculty positions for years. In addition, new doctoral programs from non-traditional programs has meant even more growth in graduates despite the low percentage of completers. You should carefully consider whether a doctoral will support your ambitions to become a professor. It might make sense to first investigate your opportunities with a master's degree teaching undergraduate courses, and once you are certain this is a path worth pursuing, then start the doctorate.

What does accreditation have to do with it?

Accreditation in higher education is a big deal. Accreditation also has many aspects that can be confusing even for people who work in the industry. Unfortunately, accreditation can have a substantial impact on the value of your educational degrees if you hope to become a professor.

In the beginning (in the early 20th century), accreditation evolved out of two needs. First, universities needed a way to know which colleges produced undergraduate students who were capable of graduate work. Later this extended to being able to identify what credits could be transferred from one institution to another. Second, professional associations (like lawyers and doctors) wanted to set standards for what people studying to join their profession should know. Eventually, the federal government used accreditation as the basis for determining what institutions could provide federal financial aid to students.

Accreditation consists of two overlapping systems. First, institutional accreditation covers the college or a university as a whole. This can either be regional or national accreditation. Regional accreditors evolved out of the early years of accreditation as a system by which colleges and universities agreed to transfer credit and accept each other's graduates for graduate school. National accreditation tends to focus on career programs including barber and cosmetology schools but also colleges offering graduate degrees in business.

In my opinion, one form of accreditation is not better than another. They serve different purposes. However, regional accreditation is more prestigious than national accreditation. Someone with a degree from a nationally accredited institution will generally not be hired by a regionally accredited school or allowed to the start a graduate program at a regionally accredited university. Both national and regional accreditation qualify an institution to offer federal financial aid.

The other system of accreditation represents the history of accreditation in professional associations. This type of accreditation focuses on specific programs within an institution. Usually it does not help with federal financial aid but in some professions, only degrees from accredited programs will be considered for licensure in that profession. In business, there are actually three different accreditors that accredit business programs. While I would not claim that any of the three are better than the others, The Association to Advance Collegiate Schools of Business (AACSB) tends to be the most prestigious. They also require their members to hire faculty who have degrees from AACSB accredited programs. If you want to teach in one of these programs, you will need to also earn a degree from one of these programs.

In summary, it is not enough to ask if a university is accredited. You will want t verify that the accreditation is from a regionally accredited institution and that the program is accredited. Not all programs have a program accreditation, and the importance varies by program, but this is something that can cause you grief later when trying to get hired.

Where should I go to grad school?

One of the common accreditation requirements for faculty is that a professor should have one degree higher than the students. A professor teaching

ndergraduates needs at least a master's degree and one teaching graduate
udents a terminal degree (usually a doctorate).

you already have a master's degree, you might be able to find a teaching
osition teaching undergraduate courses in your field of study. Community
olleges and career colleges will be primary places to look for these
opportunities. At other types of colleges and universities there may be
opportunities, but less frequently. Typically for these institutions, you will to
ave a doctoral degree.

he traditional model of graduate school was to relocate to a university and
udy on campus for 2-3 years for a master's degree and on average 10 years
 finish a doctorate (if you finished). Traditional schools think that this is a
reat model and expect their faculty to follow tradition. In the last two decades,
ough, a variety of non-traditional universities have received approval for
octoral programs. Sometimes these are PhDs, and other times they are
octorates of Business Administration or Management or Education or another
rofessional field. The only schools who care about this are the traditional
chools, and they will discount any degree that is not traditional anyway.

he quality of these degree programs varies widely. I know of at least two
rograms that are in the midst of class action lawsuits by doctoral students who
el that the university systematically made it impossible to finish. I know of
dividuals who went to these same schools with no issue, so individual results
ill vary. As someone who used to run a doctoral program, the key question is
ow many students per doctoral faculty. Even full-time faculty can only work
ith so many doctoral students at a time. When a program is oversubscribed,
culty and other resources are not available to support students effectively.
/hen I took over the doctoral program I ran, one of our first orders of business
as to increase the number of faculty and institute standardized procedures to
pport student success.

you can, a traditional residential doctoral program is best. Not only will you be
mmersed in the university for your studies, but you will have the most versatile
egree at the end. Most people cannot do that. If I had not gone straight from
y undergraduate studies into graduate school, I don't think I would have been
ble to do it later. For most people this means doing an online program. There

are a few nontraditional, face-to-face programs around mainly in psychology and education, but these are few.

In addition to looking at student to faculty ratios, you will want to look at things like accreditation and cost. For accreditation, you want regional accreditation. Programmatic accreditation even if not at the doctoral level is a good sign. That means that the school works hard to ensure it has quality in those programs, and that will spill-over.

Pricing is challenging. Anyone can calculate the cost of the courses in the program. The number of credits required and by class may vary, but the total i easy to calculate. The challenge is how much it will cost you to write the dissertation. While students in master's programs can avoid this issue, it is ver important for doctoral students. Most schools back-load the dissertation. Students take a few years knocking off courses and then suddenly they have produce this independent piece of research which can span months...costly months. The ideal is a program that integrates the research and writing into the coursework, so it is not at the end. You can make this work on your own by using papers in courses as stepping stones to your literature review in your dissertation. In research methods courses you can start designing your research. This will save you time later. The essential question, though, is how much do you need to pay each month while working on your dissertation. Ask how long it takes students to finish. Schools that are questionable will have long approval processes during the dissertation stage that will cause the process to go on longer. Watch out for those red flags.

Another factor to consider is how hard is it to get into a program. A critical aspect of graduate education is the connections you make with peers. A program with minimal admissions requirements will connect you with people who often should not be in a doctoral program, which will detract from your ow experience. Ask the school what percentage of people they admit as a way of comparing schools.

A final factor to consider is the curriculum. It will take endurance to finish any program, and you want to make sure that you are excited about most of the coursework. If you have many required courses that you dread, then you will ave a tough time getting through. Most people want to avoid statistics, but you hould have plenty of courses you are excited to take. If you don't get excited y the courses, then consider another program or whether you really want to e a professor. If you don't like the courses as a student, how are you going to ke teaching them?

Vhat teaching experience do I need to land my first eaching job?

efore someone can graduate from a K12 teaching program, she or he must rst successfully complete student teaching under the mentorship of a veteran lassroom teacher. Prior to this experience, most students have already spent significant amount of time in classrooms observing and participating in a mited fashion. This approach is intended to ensure that new teachers can in act teach.

n higher education, we do not have those same expectations. In higher ducation, the priority has always been placed on the professor's knowledge as emonstrated through research, publications, and presentations. The ssumption has been that anyone who knew there stuff well enough to earn a octorate could teach students. This is a silly idea and does not work in ractice, and it explains why so much of higher education teaching is neffective.

)ver my two decades in higher education, expectations have started to hange. Adult students pursuing higher education to advance in a professional areer are less tolerant of poor teaching than the traditional college student esh from high school. As a result, many colleges are interested in how ffective a professor is at teaching.

)uring the hiring process, hiring administrators may screen out applicants /ithout teaching experience. If you have teaching experience already, this hould not be a concern. If you are looking for that first opportunity, though, you are stuck in the land of how do I get experience if I need experience to get into the classroom?

There are a couple of things that you can do.

First, I recommend that you contact your local Chamber of Commerce or United Way to see if you can offer a class on a topic that you have expertise in. This should be something you have work experience with or have studied in graduate school. You can always do online research to fill in the gaps in your knowledge. If you offer a class for free, it is a win for the organization as they get to serve their membership with a new offering at no cost. The win for you is that you can now list this as teaching experience. (An added bonus is if you hate it, you know to not pursue any teaching opportunities.)

My career in higher ed started this way. I developed and offered classes on the World Wide Web through a local college. I was able to use the contacts developed through that experience for my first teaching position which led to a full-time position and over twenty year later a long career in higher education.

If you have concerns about public speaking, then seek out Toastmasters International. This is an incredible organization that will develop your speaking and leadership skills in a supportive environment. I have been a member, and have known others who leveraged this experience to develop their skills as a teacher. For what you receive, the dues are incredibly low.
I have known people who took courses and exams to become certified online instructors. This has never been a factor in my hiring decisions. Maybe they will help you develop your skills, and maybe other administrators value these credentials. Unless a specific school that I wanted to teach at placed value in one of these, I would not invest either the time or money.
Good schools will have faculty development programs that will help you learn to be effective in the classroom. The key is getting that first teaching opportunity and making the most of it.

Another option is to speak at a professional conference. Many disciplines have conferences for teachers and professors at both a state and national level. This is an opportunity to network with others and also to practice speaking. The etworking will introduce you to colleagues who are teaching now and can let ɔu know about openings. The speaking you can include on your cv and ːrengthen your application for teaching positions.

Questions to Consider

his chapter provided you with some general background and context on igher education and what qualifications are required to be hired as a ɪofessor. Based on this information, think about and make some notes based n these questions:

- One of the first things to do on your journey to becoming a professor is to consider what type of institution that you want to teach for and what you want to teach. What are your initial thoughts about where and what to teach?

- Based on where and what you want to teach, what are the qualifications that you feel you already possess for being a professor at this type of institution?

- Based on where and what you want to teach, what additional qualifications or experience do you think you will need to be successful at landing a teaching position?
- If you need additional education or experience, how and when are you going to get it?

he objective at this point is to develop a plan of what you will do to prepare ɔurself to be able to transform your desire to become a professor into having e qualifications to be a successful candidate.

Chapter Three: Finding and Landing a Teaching Job

Having the right educational and professional credentials provides the first ste
to becoming a professor. Next you have to have someone who is willing to giv
you an opportunity to teach. I recommend two options for finding the first and
subsequent opportunity. While the approaches here focus on part-time, adjunc
teaching opportunities, these ideas also apply to full-time positions. At many
institutions, full-time faculty are hired from the adjunct pool. Unfortunately,
many institutions do not do this and instead look beyond their existing faculty
when full-time openings occur. In many cases, this is because of the desire to
hire full-time faculty with terminal degrees when existing faculty do not have
these credentials.

Option One: The Direct Approach

So how do you find teaching opportunities? The Direct Approach is the most
common and well known and also least effective. In this approach, you apply
directly to schools that have posted an open position. On the companion web
site for the book, you can find a list of higher education websites where you ca
search for such openings.

This is a low yield strategy. Recruiters will see many resumes (CVs) for any
opening. You will need to find ways in your resume to both stand out from the
crowd but also fit into expectations.
Recruiters will be looking to see that your educational qualifications match wha
is required for the position. They will also be looking for related professional
experience. You will want to make sure that you address how your background
meets the requirements (fitting in). You will also want to highlight special
experience that you have that will make you more effective in the classroom
(standing out).
Teaching experience will often be used to screen, so make sure you highlight
your experience. If you have not taught in higher education, address other

rofessional teaching experience that you have at work or in the community. If ou don't have any, get some.

eep in mind that this is a numbers game. You might not get a hit 10% of the me. That means for every 10 applications you send out, you might get 1 terview. This is not a reflection of you exactly, but how competitive these pportunities can be. It can also take a long time to hear back. I have heard tories of people who have heard back a year after the initial application.

nline positions are the hardest because people living anywhere can apply. he quality and number of your competitors will go up as a result. Local pportunities (even for online teaching) can be easier to have success with.

Option Two: The Networking Approach

here is nothing wrong with the Direct Approach to applying for teaching ositions, but the Networking Approach provides a method that gives you reater control over the process. The Networking Approach focuses on eveloping a network of contacts in higher education with the goal of being the erson they call when they have an opening.

the Networking Approach, you will want to start by identifying colleges and epartments where you think you might want to teach. This will work better with cal colleges and universities, but the same approach can be used with online chools.

nce you have identified the school and the department, you will want to evelop a relationship with the hiring manager. This is usually someone with ie title of "Dean" or "Department Chair" depending on the size of the school.

ou can do this through a cold call. Find the person on the web site and call or mail them. You can also ask for introductions from friends. Ask people you now if they know anyone at the school and use this introduction to get introduced to the person you need to talk to. Conferences are another place where you can network.

Once you make contact, you do not want to ask for a job. This is impolite and will turn most people off. Unless someone is actually hiring at that time, the answer will be "no" and that will be the end of the relationship.

Instead, set-up an interview/meeting to understand what they are looking for when they hire faculty. Most educators love to talk about themselves and their work. This is why they became teachers. There is no obligation in providing guidance to someone who is considering pursuing a teaching career.

This informational interview does two things.

First, it helps you know what that school is looking for and whether you are a good fit or not. There is no reason to hold out hope for a school that will never hire someone with your background. It may also tell you what you need to do professionally or educationally to be a candidate in the future.

Second, it makes the hiring administrator aware of you. This is how I earned my first teaching position. The Dean needed someone to teaching one night a week at an off-campus location. Because we had already met, he called me and offered me the job.

Most of the time, a college or university will be fully-staffed. Adding a new instructor would mean taking courses away from someone else. The opportunity to start teaching arises when enrollment dictates adding a new section of a class or when an existing faculty member is no longer available. In these circumstances, an administrator has no interest in trying to find someone new especially when class starts next week. The key is being first in mind when that opportunity arises, so you receive the offer first.

Effective salespeople know that the first yes is the hardest. Getting someone to say yes to meet with you for an interview is a relatively easy yet to get. This will make it easier for them to say yes to hire you later.

ou will want to stay in touch but don't be pushy. Focus on what is happening
t their school and in their department. If someone feels that you are only
terested in a job, they will be less likely to look on you favorably.

our local community college is probably the easiest place to start. Being local,
iey will want to hire locals, and they tend to hire many part-time faculty. They
lso focus on the teaching qualifications and not on research or other
xperiences.

you are looking to teach online, you can use a search engine to look for
nline colleges and universities that offer the program that you are interested
i.

Preparing for the Application and Interview

you are applying for positions directly, you will need a cover letter and
esume as a minimum.
s with all job applications, the cover letter should be tailored to the position
nd how you meet the qualifications.

i higher education, the resume is usually known as a curriculum vitae (cv).
he cv will often be longer than a traditional resume as it should include a list of
ublications and presentations. Education should be at the front of the cv as
ducational qualifications are the most important consideration in whether
omeone is qualified for higher education teaching.

ome postings will ask for a "Teaching Philosophy." This is a personal
tatement about how you approach teaching. You will want to tailor it for the
istitution and what they value in teaching, but at the same time you will want
) be true to yourself.

strongly encourage you to purchase personal business cards with your
ontact information. Using your work business cards can be seen as a conflict

of interest as you are promoting yourself and not your employer. Also, if your employment changes, a personal business card will still be current.

On your personal contact information, use a personal email address. If by some chance you still use AOL, do not use that as your email address or people will make fun of you. A Gmail account is fine as is Outlook.com. You want something professional and permanent. I use the email address I have had since college since I get to keep it as an alumni and it won't change.

If you have an interview or are networking, having sample course materials or teaching portfolio will separate you from everyone else. Even if you have materials you have developed for a free workshop, sharing these will demonstrate your commitment in a way that most will not even think to do.

Your Digital Identity

Before you start applying for positions, as yourself is if you have anything less than professional online? You might trust Facebook's privacy controls, but I would not. People will search for you, and you would be amazed at what can be found. You will be judged based on your digital identity, and schools will be concerned about what your future students will find out about you.

If you do not have one, a LinkedIn profile is a good idea. You should complete it fully, and include a link on your cv to LinkedIn. This will allow you to demonstrate your network, recommendations from others, endorsements, and even portfolio features. The summary on your profile should be your digital elevator speech. This is an important opportunity to brand yourself.

Chapter Four: Making the Most of Your Shot

You have your first teaching job? Awesome! Now what?

There are a few tricks to make the most of your shot and to get invited back.

First, look for opportunities to volunteer to develop courses, advise students, etc. Most colleges and universities are stretched regarding resources, and volunteers from the faculty can help shoulder the burden. Sometimes this will be paid, but don't go looking for paid opportunities. The key is by serving and helping out you make yourself indispensable. I would favor a newbie who pitches in over a veteran who only teaches and leaves. This is essential if you want a full-time gig.

Second, pay attention to deadlines and due dates. The quickest way to not get invited back is to miss deadlines. Grades are due at a certain time because a bunch of other processes rely on this information. You do not want to be the sand in the gears.

Third, treat students with respect but don't try to buy affections. Students will see through it if they think you are catering to them. They wanted to be respected, which means listening and valuing their perspectives, but that does not mean giving them what they want. Administrators pay attention to how many "As" you give out, and it will be noticed if you use all of the grades in the grading scale. Noticed in a good way.

It is important to be aware that different schools will have very different levels of support for faculty in both curriculum and training.

At many schools, a new faculty member will be given a textbook and expected to develop a syllabus from scratch. Some schools might provide a course outline or a template for the course. In some cases, the faculty member will need to identify a textbook and other resources.

Most schools have some sort of orientation for new faculty. It might be as informal as a one-on-one meeting, or it might be a meeting with all faculty. Training might be provided, and in some cases, there might be a certification program. Most online universities will require new faculty to successfully complete their in-house certification program.

The key is to take advantage of every opportunity…paid or not. At worst, it will be noted that you are active in meetings and training. At best, you will learn something that will make you more effective in the classroom.

If things go well, you will be offered additional courses. Plus, once you have successfully completed your first course, you can update your cv and be better positioned to be hired at additional institutions.

You should also be prepared to fire an institution that is not working for you. Unfortunately, some schools might be ethically challenged and refuse to enforce academic standards. Other schools may have unrealistic faculty expectations in proportion to faculty pay. While many schools have effective policies and programs to support adjunct faculty, others can be chaotic. You have to make your own determination about your own personal values and when a school is not a fit for those values. Just be willing to have the courage to be the one to separate from a school that is not a good fit for you and do so with sufficient time to allow them to fill future classes with someone else.

Chapter Five: Career Advice for Future Professors

Clearly, I have my own opinions and thoughts about how to become a professor, and I want to offer the advice of others in this final chapter.

The Literature

On the companion web site, I provide links to a variety of articles I have collected over time. One of my favorites is Faculty, Don't Let Your Babies Grow Up to Be Academics by Professor Betsy Lucal. Professor Lucal recognizes the upsides to being a professor, but she also warns her own students away from this career path. In reflecting on her own career, Lucal observes that many of the positions in her department have been eliminated or converted to part-time positions. Her experience reflects larger trends in higher education. In 1975, 3% of faculty were contingent faculty including part-time faculty. Today that percentage is over 70%. (See Coming to You Soon: Uber U). I would argue that Professor Lucal's observations reflect the reality at many traditional schools.

Finding and landing a full-time, tenure track position is hard. In I Found a Tenure-Track Job. Here's What it Took, Jeremy Yoder describes the process he went through to land a position Yoder followed a very traditional path of graduate school followed by years working as a postdoctoral researcher to further establish his research portfolio. His experience his illuminating of what it took.

Dr. Erin Bartram had a less happy ending to her search for a permanent faculty position. After multiple failed searches she made the decision to leave higher education. Her story posted in her blog was covered in the Chronicle of Higher Education as an example of "quit lit." (A new genre of writing by professors giving up on the field.)

Challenges Experienced by Professors

As part of my own research to support this project, I posted a short three question survey to several groups on LinkedIn:

- Where are you in your journey to be a professor (Just starting to think about it; Looking for my first teaching gig; Seasoned veteran of the classroom)?
- Wherever you are in your journey, what are the challenges you are currently experiencing in your teaching career?
- What advice do you have for someone thinking about or just starting a career as a professor?

After three weeks, I had 344 responses (totally exceeding my expectations). The purpose of the survey was to get input into an online class I have been working on "So You Think You Want to be a Professor?". My hope was to get a better idea of the challenges faced by people looking to start a teaching career in higher education and advice from those that have taken this journey before.

While I did receive some responses from people who were just thinking about or looking for that first position, 75% of respondents were seasoned veterans. While this was not the original intent, the results provide valuable insights.

Two categories emerged from the responses regarding challenges for those just starting:

Opportunity (50%): Finding an opportunity was listed as the major challenge.

- Not even sure where to start to find a part-time/evening teaching gig. They don't seem to be advertised much on the standard job search sites
- My biggest challenge is finding a position. I find that you have to be connected to someone to get an interview.

Qualifications (21%): Having the right qualifications including the right degree or teaching experience holds many back.

- Lack of experience. Getting experience requires encountering that one person willing to take a chance on you to give you they experience.
- Most online schools want you to have numerous years of experience in teaching. This is a hindrance since I am a newbie.

The challenges from the experienced professors were more varied. Six categories cover 80% of the responses.

Students (22%): Professors describe the challenges of engaging students and working with students who themselves appear to be hardly working.

- One of the biggest challenges is continuing to find new ways to engage students who need more and more action
- Keeping students' attention and enhancing the content on a regular basis. Engagement is a key factor in teaching.

Opportunity (19%): Even experienced professors describe the challenges of finding new opportunities especially full-time positions.

- Ensuring a consistent income teaching between four universities.
- Just been made redundant and despite my experience and skills, finding it hard to get interviews. The recruitment process has become too algorithmic.

Teaching (15%): More effective teaching especially in using technology was a common concern.

- Keeping up to date with the rapidly evolving developments in learning technologies / approaches, and ensuring high quality delivery and outcomes.
- Widening participation programs always bring in learners from disparate backgrounds that have a mixed prior learning experience. This broadly speaking leads to the need to be able to cater in the classroom for

different personalities, different groups and demographics, different input and entry qualifications, etc.

Time (14%): Balancing teaching, research, and service provide a challenge, especially as expectations for all three are increasing.

- Balancing work and home. Balancing research, service and teaching commitments.
- Getting enough time to research as well as teaching and the service component of job.

Culture (8%): The culture of higher education including conflict with administrators detracts from the joys of the job.

- Toxic work environment-working in a system with a broken infrastructure with folks that want to climb the corporate ladder. Teaching to traditional college students who are challenged with how to study, and challenged in my own delivery of content as traditionally taught 25 to 30 in a classroom and now facing 75 to 100 in a classroom
- Upper administration is spinning off ideas that drastically change the academy, but they are doing it with virtually no input from faculty.

Pay (5%): A final major concern is the low pay especially in relation to the time and effort that are required.

- Over-worked and underpaid. As an Adjunct Lecturer, we are expected to work the same as a tenured Professor, but without the job security, same benefits, or comparable salary. If an Adjunct wants to secure a tenured position, he or she must bend over backwards to demonstrate that they will be willing to attend every meeting, take on administrative tasks, and lead new initiatives oftentimes for little compensation or even for free. It's very discouraging to have a Master's Degree, but make only $50k a year, where a tenured Professor would start at as low as $65k a year (one tenured Professor at my community college makes $90k a year). On top of that, we have to work at two, three, sometimes even four, different colleges or universities to make ends meet because our contracts, and the college's budget, limit the amount classes we can teach. This also takes away precious time to invest in our work, which makes securing the coveted tenure position even harder.

- Low pay--I'm currently teaching at six colleges to maintain a decent living standard. Obviously I spend a lot of time working and am on schedule to teach a total of 30 courses in 2017.

Advice for Those Starting

The advice I received from my simple survey was overwhelming in its sincerity and wisdom. I have organized the advice into several themes organized around the journey to becoming and being a professor.

Purpose (52 comments): If the why is big enough, the how will take care of itself. Your purpose in becoming a professor needs to be clear and strong to sustain you on the journey.

- It has to be founded upon a passion to help the students, that is the required intrinsic motivation. Don't do it for the title or the money, if that is the case, look into another area where you can succeed.
- If you don't love teaching, then this isn't the job for you. You have to have a passion for helping people learn and grow. The more passion you have, the better you will be at your job. Also, it doesn't matter as much as to how well you know about the subject matter as much as it matters how well you know how to TEACH said subject matter. Learn pedagogy, too! Lastly, whether you like it or not, technology matters. It's a huge part of the way students today learn and they expect it to be incorporated into the classroom. Also, most colleges and universities offer hybrid and online classes. Distance education is the future. Learn how to construct online courses and teach online. It will keep you relevant.

Negative Advice (27 comments): Many of the commentators advised staying away from a career in higher education.

- The pay is low and opportunities are few.
- Get the hell out while you still have health and sanity. Hopefully, you have not lost your family and friends while you worked on your doctorate.

Grad School (16 comments): Obtaining the required academic credentials is an important preparatory step to a career in higher ed. Typically that means a doctorate.

- Do your doctorate in something of interest, but also something that would align with job openings.
- Find a mentor who believes in you and wants you to succeed. Do not attempt a thesis under with an advisor who doesn't support you. Research the expectations at any school you are considering for either your doctoral work or a career.

Career Planning (14 comments): Commenters provided advice on how to plan one's career path for maximum effect.

- Be willing to take adjunct positions and bad hours if needed just to get experience. Be willing to teach at nearby colleges as well. I once taught at 4 different colleges and traveled 400 miles a week.
- Consider very carefully if sufficient jobs exist in your chosen field; whether or not you are willing to be adjunct/contingent faculty if there are few tenure-track or full-time positions in your field. Adjunct can be very rewarding but it usually requires other employment to provide an adequate income.

Networking (34 comments): Networking is essential to ensure that this is a profession that you want to pursue, to help you land that first job, and to develop a support network for your career including identifying a mentor.

- Begin networking networking networking, especially as a student. Also, be yourself and show your personality. Unlike corporate world, your colleagues are basically who hire you. Having a connection with them i sometimes the de facto factor, because other applicants will most likely match you professionally.

- Look to align with colleagues or leaders that you value and admire. Your capacity to do good work will be a product of the momentum that you can generate collectively and this has never been more important, in relation to sustaining oneself.

erseverance (24 comments): The journey to a higher education teaching osition follows a long road. Even after finishing your doctorate, finding that first b can be demoralizing.

- Be sure of your commitment because it is not as easy as you think it will be. It takes a great deal of time and effort but the rewards are amazing
- Have patience, and keep building your skills while trying to secure full-time employment.

eaching (96 comments): By far, the greatest number of comments were dvice on how to be effective in the classroom. Traditionally, professors were xpected to be good teachers on the basis of subject matter expertise. Today, tudents and institutions have higher expectations from faculty.

- Be sure that you that your passion lies in empowering others for success because mastery of content area does not alone make one a good professor. Both on-line and classroom teaching require engaged thinkers prepared to serve students in rapidly changing environment.
- Assuming you are sincerely involved in your discipline, above all, bring several years of professional (work) experience to your classroom. The students will recognize / appreciate your personal experience versus only what the publishing companies provide in their classroom packages.

esearch (14 comments): While many institutions do not expect faculty to onduct research, at other institutions it is a priority consideration for full-time ositions and tenure. Research especially research that generates external unding can be more important than teaching effectiveness.

- Focus on research: teaching is fun, but neither appreciated by your department nor quality controlled by any meaningful measure.

- Be sure you understand what a professor's job involves. At most R1 [research intensive] universities, profs spend most of their time searching for funding. And it isn't better at most smaller universities wh are trying to become research universities. If you love teaching, be sure to apply to a university whose primary focus is teaching!

General Advice (35 comments): General advice includes those comments that did not fit into one of the other categories.

- Choose your university carefully. Think carefully about your subject fiel and area of expertise within it. Travel, connect!
- Consider your own personality and skill set firstly. Do you feel that you have the skills that will match well with this role and will the isolated nature of the role working alone much of the time suit your work style?

Coaching

If you need personalized assistance, there are coaching and other services available. I have included links in the companion website.

Chapter Six: The Independent Professor

Why Become an Independent Professor?

In the summer of 2017, I did a survey for input on this project. I was surprised by one of the themes in the responses...how many people recommend that others not pursue becoming a professor. Even more I heard about the challenges of finding and keeping teaching positions.

At the same time, I had been studying online entrepreneurship. A large network of coaches, trainers, authors, and consultants offer courses and other services to help people share their expertise online. Very few of these gurus have any experience in formal online higher education. More often than not they take pride in their lack of academic qualifications.

I realized that on the one hand that many bright, educated, and experienced professors were searching for teaching opportunities, and on the other, many people were offering courses and other material to a wide, cash paying audience. From this was born the idea of the independent professor, the professor sharing their expertise outside of traditional higher education.

On a broader scale, formal higher education appears to be unprepared for modern society where old careers are rapidly disappearing and new careers requiring new skills are emerging. The traditional college model of "one and done" degrees is not flexible enough to meet lifelong learning needs. Independent professors have the opportunity to create value for learners that educational institutions cannot.

What is an Independent Professor?

In many creative fields, the term "indie artist" conveys a musician or a filmmaker who creates art outside of the traditional, corporate structures of music labels and studios. I think the same concept should apply to professors/scholars.

In this sense, independent professors practice scholarship and teaching outside of the traditional walls of universities and publishers.

Professors have a calling driven by two passions. First, they have a passion to become a subject matter expert in a field of knowledge whether that is art history, accounting, or something else. Second, they have a passion to share their knowledge with others.

Traditionally, colleges and universities provide the platform for professors to fulfill their callings. However, in the last twenty years, professors have found it increasingly difficult to find a stable university home. The competition for full-time positions is particularly intense, and even finding part-time opportunities can be a challenge.

In the early 1990s when the Internet and World Wide Web were first emerging I wrote about the potential of the Internet to democratize information. Historically, institutions such as universities and publishers controlled the dissemination of information because the required infrastructure like printing presses and classrooms were expensive to build. The Internet provided a path to remove these intermediaries and connect directly with an audience.

In the years since, the tools and opportunities have increased. In fact, many coaches advertise how anyone can write a book or teach a class...no advance degree required. Anyone can play baseball too, but not everyone can play at the level of the big leagues. Professors have the education and experience to be leaders in this new environment and raise the bar on the quality of what is available.

The independent professor can create their own platform to share their knowledge directly with students and others.

variety of systems are available online that allow anyone to become a teacher or publisher of information and knowledge products without having specialized technical skills or requiring buckets of money to invest.

How Do I Become an Independent Professor?

you are interested in the possibility of establishing your independence as a teacher and scholar, you have many options for creating and publishing courses. I have written about this on my blog (https://www.drcmdavis.com) and will explore this topic further in my next book.

Made in the USA
Las Vegas, NV
05 January 2024